Meet the dinosaurs

Before you start reading *Tyrannosaurus, King of the Dinosaurs*, let's meet its main characters. Who are they? What do they look like? And where did they live?

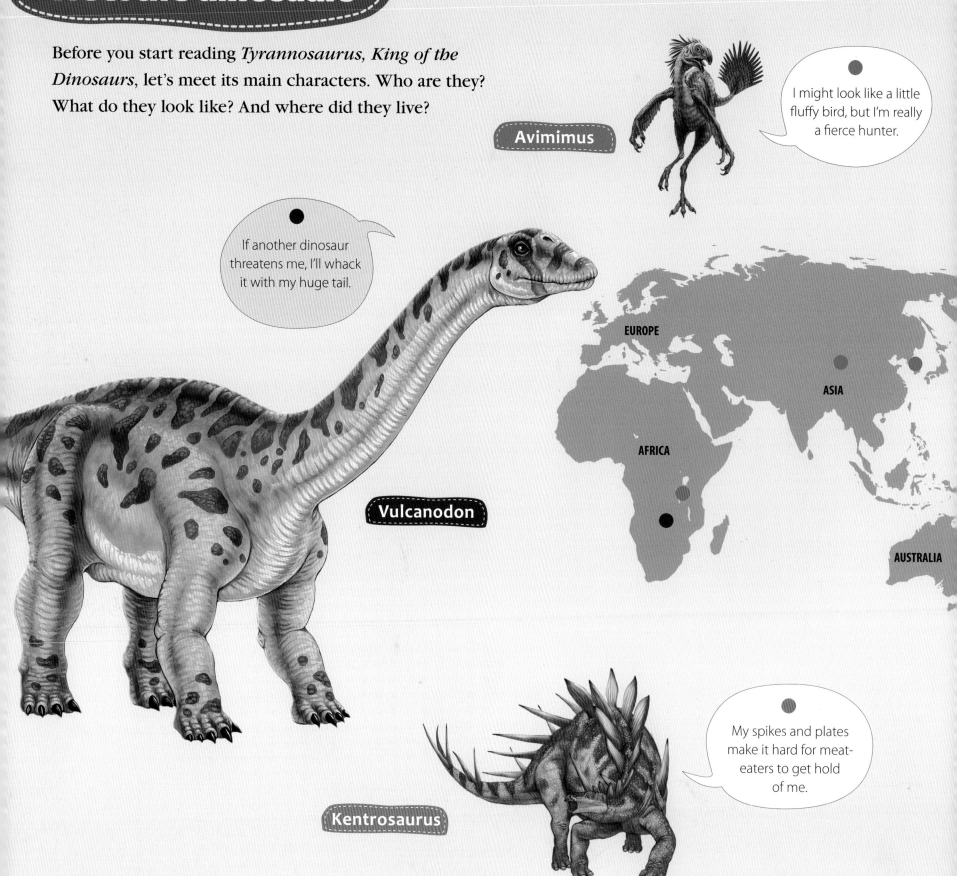

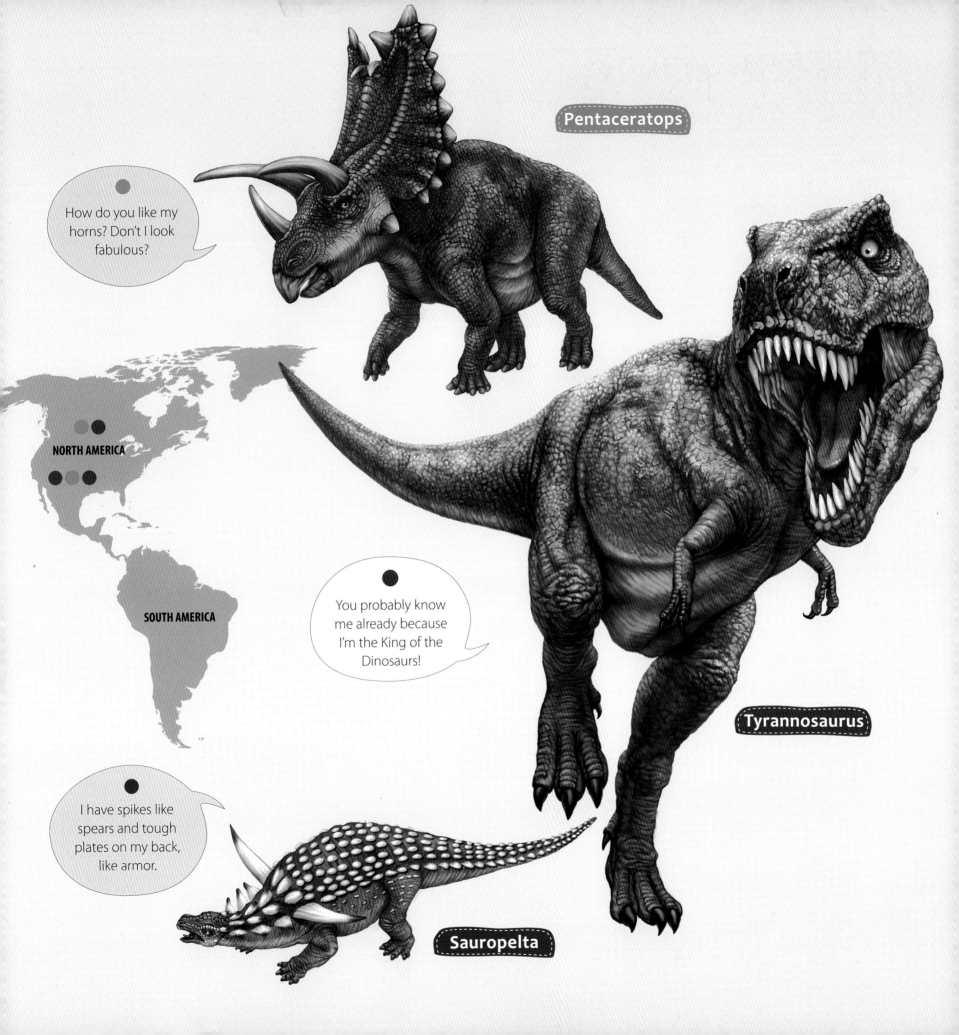

big & SMALL

Original Korean text and illustrations by Dreaming Tortoise
Korean edition © Aram Publishing

This English edition published by big & SMALL in 2016
by arrangement with Aram Publishing
English text edited by Scott Forbes
English edition © big & SMALL 2016

Distributed in the United States and Canada by
Lerner Publishing Group, Inc.
241 First Avenue North
Minneapolis, MN 55401 U.S.A.
www.lernerbooks.com

Photo credits:
Page 28, bottom: © Lee Ruk

ISBN: 978-1-925248-78-4
Printed in Korea

To learn about dinosaur fossils, see page 28.
For information on the main groups of dinosaurs,
see the Dinosaur Family Tree on page 30.

Tyrannosaurus
King of the Dinosaurs

Tyrannosaurus

big & SMALL

Vulcanodon

SAY IT:
Vul-KAH-no-don

A young Vulcanodon was feeding in the forest with its mother.
The Vulcanodons stretched their long necks up into the trees
and pulled leaves off the branches.
To reach even higher, they rose up
on their back legs.

LENGTH: 20–23 feet
(6–7 meters)

HEIGHT: 8 feet
(2.5 meters)

WEIGHT: 5.5–7.7 tons
(5–7 tonnes)

WHEN IT LIVED:	TRIASSIC	JURASSIC	CRETACEOUS

GROUP: Sauropods

DIET: Plants

WHERE IT LIVED:
Africa
(Zimbabwe)

Vulcanodon's name means "the volcano's tooth."
It was given this name because the first
Vulcanodon remains, or fossils, were found
in an area with many volcanoes.

The Vulcanodons went for a walk along the river.
Suddenly the young one sensed danger.
He called out in alarm — and just in time!
The mother saw a group of Megapnosaurus approaching.
She swung her large tail and sent one of them flying.
That was enough to scare them off!

Vulcanodon had a small head with large, strong teeth.
These teeth were good for chewing bark and leaves.
Sometimes Vulcanodon also ate stones!
The stones rolled about in its stomach
and mashed the leaves it had eaten.
This helped it digest its food.

MEGAPNOSAURUS
GROUP: Theropods
DIET: Meat
WHEN IT LIVED: Late Triassic
to early Jurassic
WHERE IT LIVED: Africa (Zimbabwe)
LENGTH: 6.6 feet (2 meters)
HEIGHT: 5 feet (1.5 meters)
WEIGHT: 33 pounds
(15 kilograms)

Kentrosaurus

SAY IT:
Ken-tro-SAW-rus

CERATOSAURUS

GROUP: Theropods
DIET: Meat
WHEN IT LIVED: Late Jurassic
WHERE IT LIVED: Africa (Tanzania),
North America (USA)
LENGTH: 20–33 feet (6–10 meters)
HEIGHT: 8 feet (2.5 meters)
WEIGHT: 1.1 tons
(1 tonne)

A pair of Kentrosaurus were nibbling
on some ferns in a corner of a swamp.
Suddenly they heard a tremendous roar.
A massive Ceratosaurus was charging toward them.
The Kentrosaurus turned and pointed their spiky
tails toward the attacker, stopping it in its tracks.

Ceratosaurus means "horned lizard."
This dinosaur's body was covered with
bony plates and spiky, horn-like ridges.

ALLOSAURUS

GROUP: Theropods
DIET: Meat
WHEN IT LIVED: Late Jurassic
WHERE IT LIVED: North America (USA),
Europe (Portugal), Africa (Tanzania), Australia
LENGTH: 25–40 feet (7.5–12 meters)
HEIGHT: 10–13 feet (3–4 meters)
WEIGHT: 1.6–3.3 tons
(1.5–3 tonnes)

LENGTH: 13–16.5 feet
(4–5 meters)

HEIGHT: 6.6 feet
(2 meters)
WEIGHT: 1.1–1.7 tons
(1–1.5 tonnes)

WHEN IT LIVED:	TRIASSIC	JURASSIC	CRETACEOUS
GROUP: Stegosaurs		DIET: Plants	

WHERE IT LIVED:

Africa
(Tanzania)

Kentrosaurus was a gentle plant-eater. The spikes on its tail were up to 12 inches (30 centimeters) long. They were usually enough to make predators like Ceratosaurus and Allosaurus think twice about attacking.

Large numbers of Kentrosaurus fossils have been found together. This suggests this dinosaur usually lived in large groups or herds.

Pentaceratops

SAY IT:
Pen-ta-SER-ra-tops

An adult Pentaceratops heard the thump of footsteps. Its eyes widened in terror as it realized it and its baby were being attacked by a fearsome predator, Albertosaurus.

It turned around to face its enemy and pointed its three long horns at Albertosaurus. It would do whatever it could to protect its young.

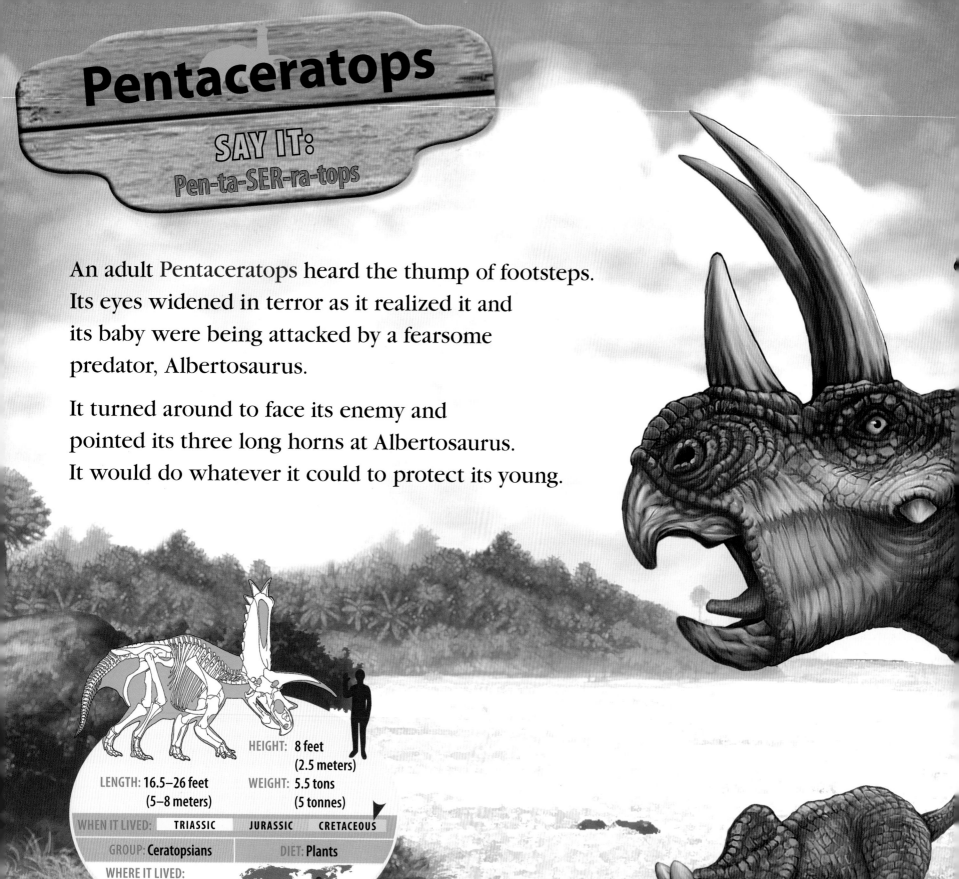

HEIGHT: 8 feet
(2.5 meters)

LENGTH: 16.5–26 feet
(5–8 meters)

WEIGHT: 5.5 tons
(5 tonnes)

WHEN IT LIVED:	TRIASSIC	JURASSIC	CRETACEOUS

GROUP: Ceratopsians	DIET: Plants

WHERE IT LIVED:
North America
(USA, Canada)

The name Pentaceratops means "five-horned face." The dinosaur was given this name because as well as its three horns it had two small spikes on its cheeks.

Tyrannosaurus

SAY IT:
Tie-ran-no-SAW-rus

The Tyrannosaurus charged, their huge jaws open and their long teeth glinting in the sun. The herd of Hypacrosaurus scattered in all directions, fleeing in panic.

The full name of Tyrannosaurus is *Tyrannosaurus rex*. The first word means "tyrant lizard" in Greek (a tyrant is a cruel ruler) and *rex* means "king." Terrifying Tyrannosaurus was truly the King of the Dinosaurs!

HEIGHT: 20 feet (6 meters)

LENGTH: 40–43 feet (12–13 meters)

WEIGHT: 6.6–7.7 tons (6–7 tonnes)

WHEN IT LIVED: TRIASSIC JURASSIC CRETACEOUS

GROUP: Theropods

DIET: Meat

WHERE IT LIVED: North America (USA, Canada)

Sprinting across the clearing,
a Tyrannosaurus quickly caught
up with one of Hypacrosaurus.
It seized it in its sharp claws and
opened its fearsome jaws …

HYPACROSAURUS

GROUP: Ornithopods
DIET: Plants
WHEN IT LIVED: Late Cretaceous
WHERE IT LIVED: North America
(Canada, USA)
LENGTH: 23–30 feet (7–9 meters)
HEIGHT: 10 feet (3 meters)
WEIGHT: 3.3–4.4 tons
(3–4 tonnes)

Tyrannosaurus had massively powerful jaws. These helped it crunch up the bones of its prey. Its teeth were very long and very sharp, and could easily slice through flesh.

19

Avimimus

SAY IT:
Ah-vee-MY-mus

A Meganeura, a giant dragonfly, flew across a clearing. Suddenly a creature like a large bird leaped up and snatched it from the air. The hunter wasn't a bird, however. It was Avimimus, a small dinosaur.

Avimimus was like a small ostrich.
It had a large beak, but no teeth.
Its body was covered with feathers and
it moved around on its slender back legs.

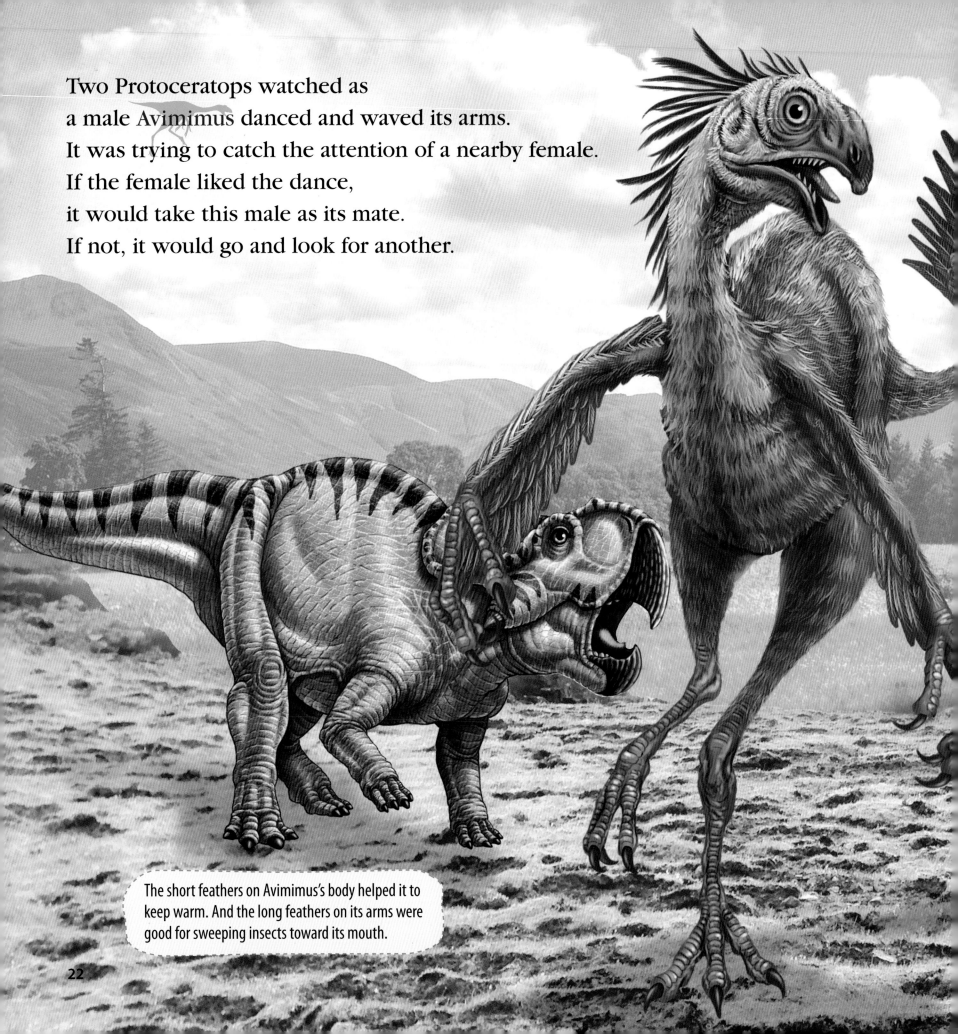

Two Protoceratops watched as
a male Avimimus danced and waved its arms.
It was trying to catch the attention of a nearby female.
If the female liked the dance,
it would take this male as its mate.
If not, it would go and look for another.

The short feathers on Avimimus's body helped it to keep warm. And the long feathers on its arms were good for sweeping insects toward its mouth.

HEIGHT:	**3.3 feet (1 meter)**
LENGTH: **5 feet (1.5 meters)**	WEIGHT: **33–55 pounds (15–25 kilograms)**

WHEN IT LIVED: **TRIASSIC** **JURASSIC** **CRETACEOUS**

GROUP: **Theropods**   DIET: **Insects, lizards**

WHERE IT LIVED: **Asia** (China, Mongolia)

PROTOCERATOPS

GROUP: Ceratopsians
DIET: Plants
WHEN IT LIVED: Late Cretaceous
WHERE IT LIVED: Asia (China, Mongolia, Korea)
LENGTH: 5–6.5 feet (1.5–2 meters)
HEIGHT: 3.3 feet (1 meter)
WEIGHT: 530 pounds (240 kilograms)

Sauropelta

Two Sauropeltas were quietly munching on plants. Because they were short, these dinosaurs usually ate low-growing plants like ferns.

24

Sauropelta was nearly as big as a bus.
Its huge body was covered in thick, bony plates,
and it had long spikes like spears on its shoulders.
This made it hard for predators to attack.

HEIGHT: 6 feet
(1.8 meters)

LENGTH: 16.5–26 feet
(5–8 meters)

WEIGHT: 3 tons
(2.8 tonnes)

WHEN IT LIVED: TRIASSIC   JURASSIC   CRETACEOUS

GROUP: Ankylosaurs   DIET: Plants

WHERE IT LIVED:
North America
(USA)

A group of Deinonychus began moving
toward the Sauropeltas. The adult
Sauropeltas did not run but simply
lay flat on the ground.

The upper part of Sauropelta's body was well protected.
But its underside was softer, and easier for attackers to hurt.
So when Sauropelta was in danger,
lying down was the best way
to protect itself.

DEINONYCHUS

GROUP: Theropods
DIET: Meat
WHEN IT LIVED: Early Cretaceous
WHERE IT LIVED: North America (USA)
LENGTH: 10–12 feet (3–3.5 meters)
HEIGHT: 4 feet (1.2 meters)
WEIGHT: 175–220 pounds
(80–100 kilograms)

Dinosaur Fossils

Fossils are the remains of dinosaurs. They can be hard parts of dinosaurs, such as bones and teeth, that have slowly turned to stone. Or they may be impressions of bones, teeth, or skin preserved in rocks.

▲ Model of a Vulcanodon

Vulcanodon

The first Vulcanodon fossil was found in Zimbabwe in Africa in 1969. In 1972, the dinosaur was named by scientist Michael Raath. Big dagger-like teeth were found with the Vulcanodon fossils, so at first the scientists thought this dinosaur was a meat-eater. But now they know that the teeth belonged to a different dinosaur!

Kentrosaurus

In the early 1900s, German scientists led several expeditions to look for dinosaur fossils in Africa. Kentrosaurus was one of the dinosaurs these expeditions discovered. German dinosaur hunter Edwin Henning used the fossils to create a full-size replica of a Kentrosaurus skeleton. He put it on display in a museum in Germany. Unfortunately, the skeleton was destroyed when a bomb landed on the museum during the World War II.

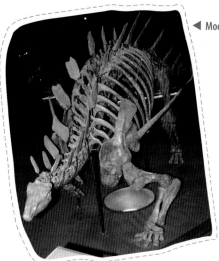

◀ Model of a Kentrosaurus skeleton

Pentaceratops

Fossils of Pentaceratops were first discovered by Charles Hazelius Sternberg in New Mexico, USA, in 1921. In 1923, dinosaur expert Henry Fairfield Osborn studied the fossils and gave the dinosaur its name. Scientists later made a full-size model of Pentaceratops, which can still be seen in the New Mexico Museum of Natural History and Science, New Mexico, USA.

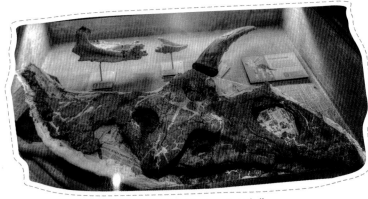

▲ Fossilized Pentaceratops skull

▶ Model of a Tyrannosaurus skeleton

Tyrannosaurus

American dinosaur hunter Barnum Brown found several Tyrannosaurus fossils at Hell Creek, Montana, USA, in 1902, and the dinosaur was named by US scientist Henry Fairfield Osborn in 1905. Since then dinosaur hunters have found many almost-complete skeletons of Tyrannosaurus. These spectacular fossils, and the fact that Tyrannosaurus was such a terrifying hunter, have made it the most famous dinosaur of all.

Avimimus

Russian scientist Sergei Kurzanov found the first fossils of Avimimus in Mongolia in 1981. He noticed several signs that this dinosaur may have had feathers, including small knobs on the arm bones to which the feathers would have been attached. Some scientists found it hard to believe that dinosaurs could have had feathers. But since then other dinosaur fossils – have proved that many dinosaurs did indeed have feathers.

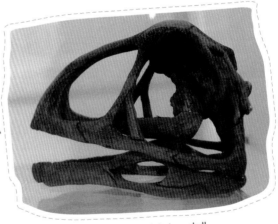

▲ Replica of an Avimimus skull

▲ Fossilized back plate and tail of a Sauropelta

Sauropelta

Barnum Brown discovered the first Sauropelta fossils in the early 1930s, in Montana. But the fossils were too small and too few for him to identify the dinosaur's group or give it a name. Thirty years later another scientist, John Ostrom, from the Peabody Museum at Yale University, USA, found an almost-complete skeleton of the same dinosaur. He gave it the name Sauropelta, meaning "shield lizard."

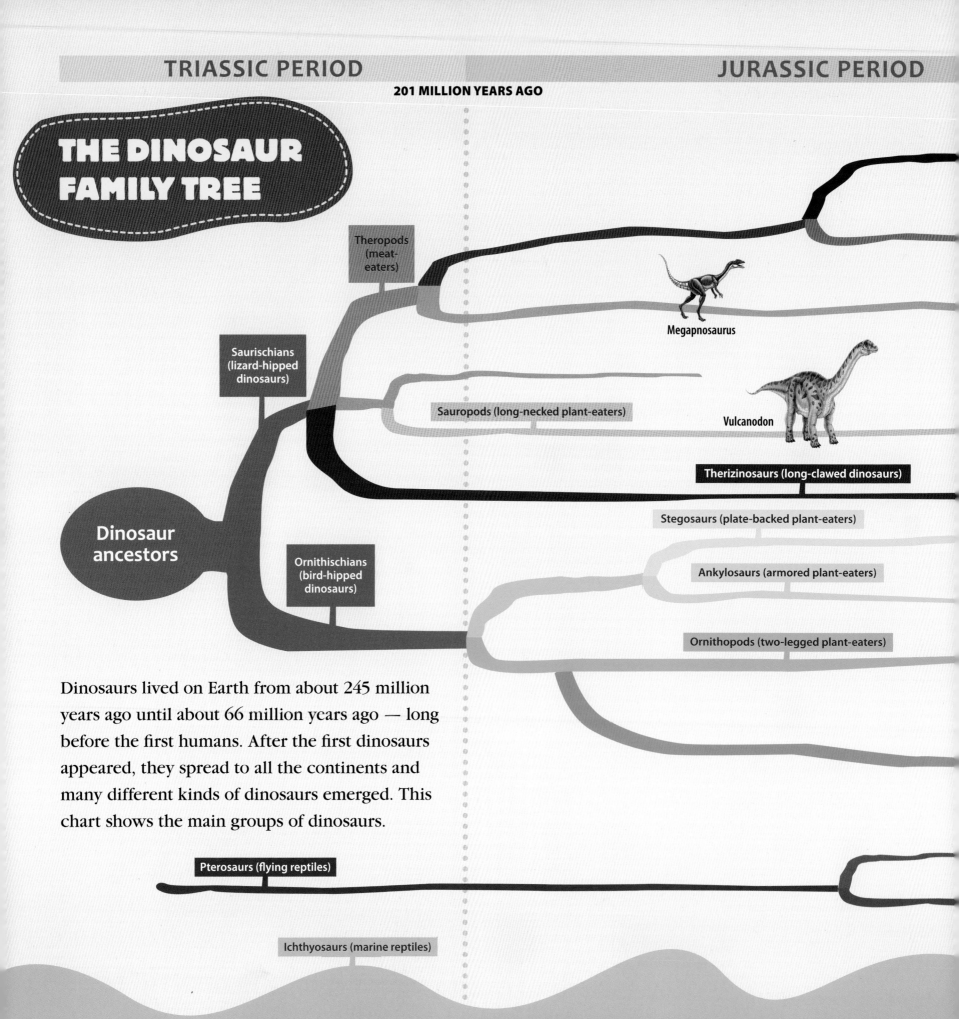

THE DINOSAUR FAMILY TREE

Theropods (meat-eaters)

Megapnosaurus

Saurischians (lizard-hipped dinosaurs)

Sauropods (long-necked plant-eaters)

Vulcanodon

Therizinosaurs (long-clawed dinosaurs)

Stegosaurs (plate-backed plant-eaters)

Dinosaur ancestors

Ankylosaurs (armored plant-eaters)

Ornithischians (bird-hipped dinosaurs)

Ornithopods (two-legged plant-eaters)

Dinosaurs lived on Earth from about 245 million years ago until about 66 million years ago — long before the first humans. After the first dinosaurs appeared, they spread to all the continents and many different kinds of dinosaurs emerged. This chart shows the main groups of dinosaurs.

Pterosaurs (flying reptiles)

Ichthyosaurs (marine reptiles)

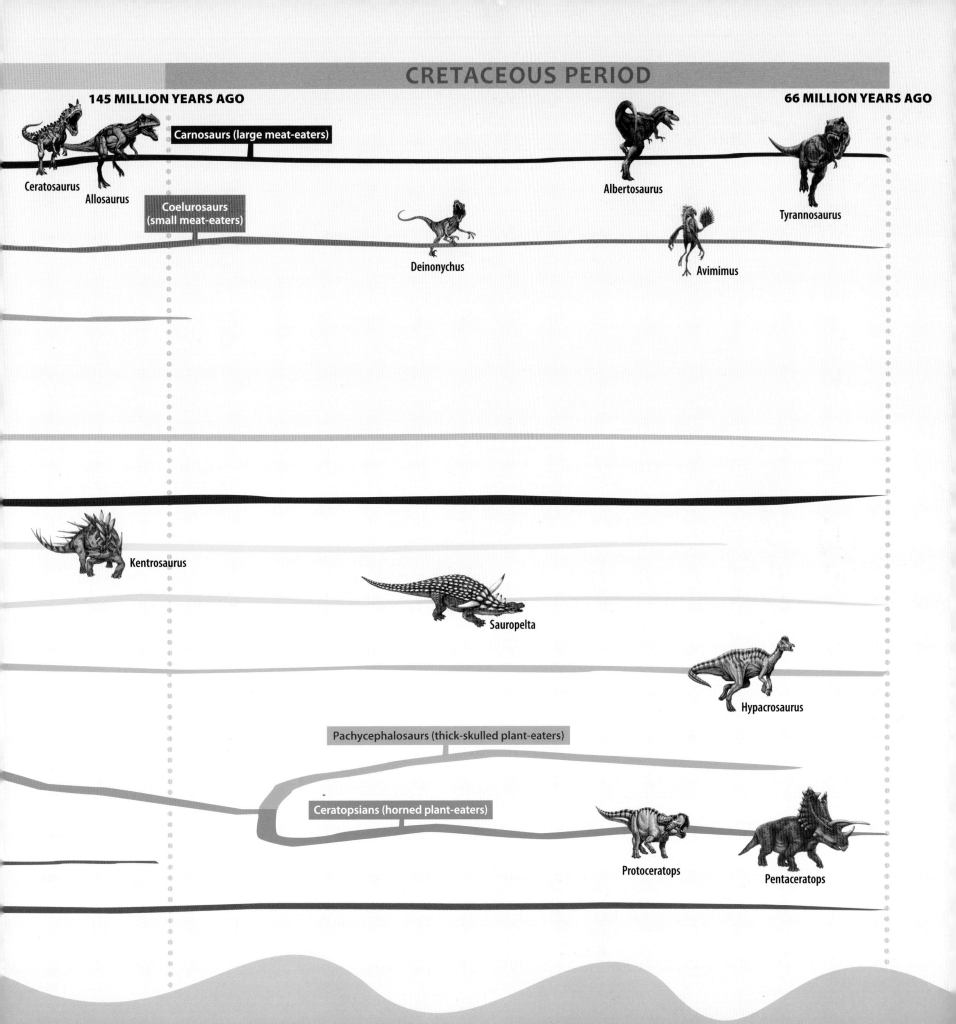

145 MILLION YEARS AGO

66 MILLION YEARS AGO

Carnosaurs (large meat-eaters)

Ceratosaurus

Allosaurus

Albertosaurus

Tyrannosaurus

Coelurosaurs (small meat-eaters)

Deinonychus

Avimimus

Kentrosaurus

Sauropelta

Hypacrosaurus

Pachycephalosaurs (thick-skulled plant-eaters)

Ceratopsians (horned plant-eaters)

Protoceratops

Pentaceratops